THE BODY FAMILY

THE BODY FAMILY

HOPE WABUKE

Haymarket Books
Chicago, Illinois

Published in 2022 by
Haymarket Books
P.O. Box 180165
Chicago, IL 60618
773-583-7884
www.haymarketbooks.org
info@haymarketbooks.org

ISBN: 978-1-64259-697-7

Distributed to the trade in the US through Consortium Book Sales and Distribution (www.cbsd.com) and internationally through Ingram Publisher Services International (www.ingramcontent.com).

This book was published with the generous support of Lannan Foundation and Wallace Action Fund.

Special discounts are available for bulk purchases by organizations and institutions. Please email info@haymarketbooks.org for more information.

Cover design by Jamie Kerry.
Cover art: *Dancing in One Spot, Number 6* by Ashon Crawley.

Printed in Canada by union labor.

Library of Congress Cataloging-in-Publication data is available.

10 9 8 7 6 5 4 3 2 1

For my father, for my mother, with overflowing thankfulness and love.

The Christian Bible has long been used to justify violences against Black people. From the middle of the sixteenth century until the middle of the twentieth century, Great Britain and then the United States used the Christian Bible to justify the theft, enslavement, and oppression of Africans and African Americans. The Christian Bible has also been used to justify the oppression of women and the violation of those of us who are both Black and woman, gender nonconforming, or nonbinary. The legacies of these oppressions persist today. *The Body Family* is an attempt to reclaim my spirituality and culture by interrogating this history of racial and gender-based violence written on our bodies and our culture—specifically colonialism, person-theft & enslavement, and genocide.

I have been a stranger in a strange land.

—Exodus 2:2, The Christian Bible

CONTENTS

I.

If Not David   3

: Goliath   5

Tongue   7

Mouth   8

Exodus: Father's American Superheroes   9

Breath   10

Job (Survivor's Guilt)   11

And after the War They Still Dream of Things Like
Angels That Shield Men from the Firing   12

Naomi after the War   14

Lamentations   15

Refugee Mind   17

The Chronicles (of a Violence Foretold)   18

II.

Figure 1: Portrait of Ruth Understanding What Became
of Eve in the Garden as Her Own Body as War
Materials: Wind & Sand   25

And after the War the Women and Girls Are Still Trying to Forget 28

Numbers   29

Genesis (First Daughter's Birth)   31

Mother after the War
Is Still Talking to the Dead   32

Proverbs of My Father's Village   34

Judges   35

Deuteronomy 37

Leviticus 38

Stomach 40

Ears 41

First & Second Crowns: A Reverse Pantoum for Two Voices 43

Blood 45

Acts of Erasure in the Country of Nameless Women 46

Rib 48

Legs 49

Figure 2: Mary, Called Girl *Materials: Blood & Darkness* 50

Figure 3: La Pièta
Materials: Breath & Air 52

Figure 4: Pièta II, Black Body as Crucifix Patterned with a Field
of Skittles Crossed with Seven-UP against a Blood Red Sky
Materials: White Concrete & Lead 53

III.

Figure 5: Pièta III, after I Watch the Video of White Woman Amy
Cooper Channeling Carolyn Bryant Donhom in Central Park in
New York City I Have a Nightmare and Wake in Cold Sweat
because All I Can See Is Your Broken Six-Year-Old Face Smashed
in Pulped and Bloody Like Emmett Till's
Materials: History & Fear 59

Mouth II 60

Figure 6: The Nameless Women as a Category in ABC's *Jeopardy!*:
A Partial List
Materials: Echo & Sound 61

Figure 7: The Nameless Women as a Category in ABC's *Jeopardy!*:
Appendix Answer Key
Materials: Erasure & Loss 63

Figure 8: Ruth as the Nameless Black Girls and Women Who Flew
because They Could Not Swim across the Water of the Middle Passage
in the Late 18th Century When Thrown Overboard, Alive and Chained,

from British Slave Ships for Collection of the Insurance Money by British Captains Who Had Done the Same to Their Animal Cargoes without Any Legal Repercussions and Thought They Could Do the Same to Human Beings because Black and Therefore Not Human or Even Animal but Only Things/Cargo as Remembered by Those Who Survived Enslavement for Generations in America and Still Remain the Accepted Prey of White Men with Guns Who Sometimes Have Badges
Materials: Unknown   64

Breath II   65

Breath III   67

Breath IV   69

Skin: The Only Black Girl in School   70

Figure 9: Ruth as a Black Girl Walking among the Nameless Black Women Disappeared Between 1619 and the Present by Great Britain and the Americas
Materials: Echo & Sound   73

Figure 10: Self-Portrait as Ruth
Materials: Unknown   76

IV.

Exodus II: Survivor's Walk   79

Figure 11: Self-Portrait as Fire and Oshun
Materials: Water   80

PiÈta IV: Revelations   81

Figure 12: Portrait of Black Jesus
as the Naming of the Ghosts
Materials: Water & Memory   85

NOTES   87

ACKNOWLEDGMENTS   91

I.

You want me to tell what was never mine to tell.
—Juliane Okot-Bitek, *100 Days*

IF NOT DAVID

when the British came
   they brought their guns

& their Jesus   they took
   our oil & our diamonds   they sent

our men to fight
   their wars in Europe   did not
     send their bodies home

Amin was eighteen
   he learned his lesson well:
      kill the other
      take what is his

when Amin & his cronies
   drove the British   out

our country   chaos
   votes ignored already
     Amin's killings were called simply

       a natural byproduct
       of events

    his buddy Obote
      the new president promoted
       him said *kill more*

    but later when Amin's killings grew too much &
   his buddy Obote said *stop*

Amin went after him too
   took the throne
    & laughed

no one can run he said
faster than a bullet

at times so many dead
    bodies were thrown
        into the Nile River the
            water stopped flowing

            Hitler Amin was fond of saying
            had the right idea

: GOLIATH

names given: His Excellency Idi Amin
    the Butcher of Uganda

                Conqueror of the British Empire
                  in Africa & Uganda in particular

     Field Marshal Al Hadji Doctor
     Big Daddy

          President for Life
          Lord of All

          the Beasts of the Earth
       & Fishes of the Sea

                       weight: 250 height: 6'4"

      what his former British commanders said: *a splendid type*
a good rugby player

          and: *a reliable soldier*
    cheerful   *energetic*

           and: *an incredible person who certainly*
    isn't mad

                 first instance of torture:
                 1962 Turkana massacre
                   (burying alive, beating to
death, etc.) overlooked promoted
    to head of armed forces: 1963

awards: Distinguished Service
Order   Victorious
Cross Military Cross.
Doctor of Law

seizes power: (backed by Israel & Great
Britain) 1971

number of wives: 4 mistresses: 30
abused: 34

number of soldiers employed in special
death squads: 18,000

number of villages wiped out: unknown

kill count: 300,000
or: 1 in 26 people

special focus: educated, Christians

flees: to Libya in 1979 after losing war

with Tanzanian forces &
Ugandan dissidents

motto: *in any country there must be*
people who have to die

TONGUE

once she saw him
    Idi Amin   my mother   he pushed

the elevator door open   pushed himself around her
    & said she was beautiful

      he said *I want you*
      he said *I have been watching*

            you he said *you will be coming*
            with me

            you like it don't you
            he said & she would have

pressed body into corner   pressed
 down the sounding

of the refusal that would
    mean death waited

      for that still silent bell to sound
      her chance to escape

      her chance at life

MOUTH

they pack nothing
to escape

detection

one change
of clothes

no books
furniture or
photographs

sewn into
their clothes:

my father's lab
specimens

my mother's
wedding ring

a day trip
with our daughter

they will say
at the border

we will be
right back

EXODUS: FATHER'S AMERICAN SUPERHEROES

because certain death
　　because genocide

he leads them out—

　　　　he is Moses, then
　　　　　Jeremiah

　　when
no one
　　else would
try

　　　　the faith to move
　　　　　mountains
　　　　& get

　　　　　to America

keep them secret
　　keep them safe

　　raise up his body
family
　　begin again

BREATH

they never speak

       of the dead   the massacres

          at school   friends

            and family   disappeared

       how they got

          word they were next

   the crossing to   Kenya

then

     America

      what happened

      in the after

      to the

  left

JOB (SURVIVOR'S GUILT)

& in the denial of the words   I know how   as latexwrapped
fingers press close to see inside   grandmother will press lips tight
together   grandmother will press sickness sounds down deep
deep down   to push back the rising of aunt's voice   throat cut bled
out by latex-gloved hands   back home in Amin's war   until the
sound rings out in tiny brown bead shapes rung round brown skin
& grandmother will press fingers soft to one   all a silent hail Mary
a silent grace

AND AFTER THE WAR THEY STILL DREAM OF THINGS LIKE ANGELS THAT SHIELD MEN FROM THE FIRING

it is only the lack
  of heat the lack of singed

skin & hair ashed
  to fill the nostrils in

the coolness of the dewed
  morning air below the unfurled

sounding of their winged
  rhythm rippling the air unfired

that is remembered

  this the stuff of miracles
that dreams are made of

we never talk of how
  now they run from flame

how they cannot cook dinner
  how they cannot see any color but red

eyes stinging memory
  closed the inferno still blazes

& they hear the cackling sizzle
  & they think they see their skin

blackening pulled from
  their bones like a

chicken on a spit crisped
    from the firing in

these night sweats
    & shivered terrors

these fever dreams
    constant &

enflamed in this still
    loudening echo

NAOMI AFTER THE WAR

when your grandchildren listen
   your mouth is alien
      foreign waters lapping at
        a foreign shore

   we have only the language of
the conquerors

within   just one small island:
   khuhu   *khuhu*

your name
   repeated becomes
     a song

LAMENTATIONS

send me home
    grandmother says

after one year in America
    i miss the orphans

the children of
    my children

disappeared in the war
    send me home

grandmother says
    i do not want to die

in a foreign land
    send me home

they are stealing
    my goats & chickens

my milk & my cows
    they are digging up my earth

my crops   my seed pulled up
    all broken   all destroyed

send me home
    but father does not

& we do not
    understand   kept silent

from anything
    to do with that home

he will not
    let us know

REFUGEE MIND

they thought
    the leaving

would be like the banyan tree
    rising   to spread wide
branches turned down become
    root again   grow new life

but there is work
    that must be done

to connect deep &
    strong   inside alien ground
you must speak   you must let yourself be known
    by these new children in all your glorious

tangled mess of becoming   your culture also
    burrow down deep in this else

     for there are always storms coming
rootless   apart you break

THE CHRONICLES (OF A VIOLENCE FORETOLD)

I. 1977

because they do not want *those niggers next door.*
   how the rocks our American neighbors hurl
      through our windows just miss
breaking the small bones of my sisters' bodies

                    all the many tiny pieces of glass
                        embedded into brown skin

     & these Midwestern doctors have said
like our minister who came over yesterday
     & would not sit on our couch:
your kind is not welcome here
   we will not treat you

     she used to be a nurse   with
     her eyebrow tweezers
my mother pulls each shard out
     one by one

they look like bloodied diamonds

II. 1994

father & I shopping
     for my middle school graduation dress until
we are asked to leave the store
     in Los Angeles
        because   your *presence*
           is making the white people uncomfortable

        my sister stealing my yellow
        cheerleading pompons on her head   swinging around
     because she is not allowed to get a weave
& she wants to *be pretty*

with *good hair*
    hair that will *move*

father's hesitation heavy
    his accented English always saying *here*
      when asked   *where are you from?*

III. 1984

the machine guns of the soldiers
    who force themselves between my sisters
      in the back seat of the car
father has rented at the Mbale Airport force
    my father to drive

              all day
               they shoot
             their guns
               out the windows
             laughing—

afterward how none of us are allowed to visit home

IV. 2014

my seventeen-month-old son running
    arms out to leap
    onto my mother & hug
every other weekend
    during the year we live
at the domestic violence shelter

V. 1930

my grandmother as a girl
    kept home from school so she will not
      be kidnapped raped

VI. 1976

the day Amin's soldiers shoot up
   my parent's classroom
     & they are spared

  in the afterward when
they shoot up the village of my body
   family when mother & father get word
      you are next

               the border crossing
            the American visa
               that precious thing
            that rarest bird of all

VII. 1988

the scar on my knee
   from the white girl
     in second grade who
calls me *nigger* & pushes
   me off the swings

VIII. 1985

my mother's years of silence
   between my older brother's death
& my younger brother's birth

  father's silence to her

IX. 2011

the old woman I see on the bus
   to school each morning
with mismatched brown & beige skin
   from a lifetime's use of lightening creams

X. 2013

    my youngest sister phoning her boyfriend
laughing that mine has said he will kill me
    that my son & I have run
& she will call my ex
    & tell him where we are hiding

            the black eye
          he has given her for their seven
          year anniversary blooms
            like a dead thing
          on her brown skin

II.

Her hands are a civil war / a refugee camp behind each ear.
　　—Warsan Shire, *Teaching My Mother How to Give Birth*

FIGURE 1: PORTRAIT OF RUTH UNDERSTANDING WHAT BECAME OF EVE IN THE GARDEN AS HER OWN BODY AS WAR
MATERIALS: WIND & SAND

how you still need
to believe it was for the love

and not its opposite   for to love
is to hold your heart outside

your body and inside
another the red echo pulsing

through your marrow to sound
what cannot be heard

                    you pulled
                        through the bones
                    by his desire

                    your clay self–molded
                        into the fitted shape
                    of his desires

this is how we make   the things our children inherit   how
that first night the man returns clutching his weapons baptized
in the bones & the blood of the animals   whose care you are
tasked with   & the man holds you down & he—
& you stay   because you were made to honor & obey
& you both know the man will do it again & he does & you stay

and the one in your belly you do not
    yet know exists is already
learning there are only two choices:
    predator and prey

see red   see nothing   swollen
   his sweat dripped into your slitted
eyes   hold onto the sting of his salt against
   your skin and know we will be legion
in the iterations of the becoming through
   your belly—we are the belly of
the belly   repeated   infinite
formed in the vast
   blackness of space   wombed
bones stuttered into being like stars

                                    night always   his arrival   pulse racing   *run*

   in the wanting to be safe was believing the first man
   who said his body would stand between the world and yours
   like your god promised   when gifting you   left anyway
   to stand alone & evicted body swelled   with child
   & you would have understood his curse was not in the pain
   of birth but   for us the afterward line with another & the next
   it would be this singular weight   this rib of unboned promise
   now shattered   to bear the ripping apart of the act of creation
   alone as what is written inside the body cannot be denied

and perhaps the anger was not in the failed test of the apple but that in
giving you the act of creation you were made his equal not the man

but how in the breaking

everything you gave

will be used

against you

                              but why would love set up love to fail?

and if there is no memory of before violence
    was learned as love   there is
only the sounding of how   long before this
    growing is a wish inside your body
there will be no warning to
    know how others   much later
will seek out this cracking sounding of
    the fault lines in our bones with
the careful deliberation of a stormed wind moving
    across not just the waters
sand or mud but the hardest   deepest rock
    to shatter further
and destroy

AND AFTER THE WAR THE WOMEN AND GIRLS ARE STILL TRYING TO FORGET

what cannot be
looked at is

held inside &
secreted within:

edged shadows like
a haunting

a drawer-sunken sweater
thought lost until

unearthed once yearly &
feeling

unraveled to remember
the breaking of threads

the warm blood
the rough object of its making

the softness of
the growth—

until the afterward—
endings looped

each needle's
yarned

& mended:
a new becoming

knit & pearl
into the absence within

NUMBERS

mother makes the doll
    after the baby boy

who would have been
    my older brother

dies   she sews his bits
    of curly black hair on top

pricks his finger with
    her needle   paints his blood

on the cotton stuffed face two
    circles for eyes   two lines

for nose & mouth
    & she is finished

all the time father
    is away she will hold baby boy

doll & hum the many melodies
    she learned to sing when

a hospital nurse back home
    in Amin's war to the skin thin

shivering ribcaged infants   tiny
    orphaned fists flailing

to eat their last
    bits of feces that would not keep

them alive another day   the lightness
    of their bodies in her arms no

heavier than the breath
of air that was her song

GENESIS (FIRST DAUGHTER'S BIRTH)

given breath
   given form

she is so beautiful   (your creation)
   & you

will love her
   because she is   yours

soft & warm
   & nice smelling

& that
   is   enough

MOTHER AFTER THE WAR
IS STILL TALKING TO THE DEAD

father says mother is forgiven
   it is okay the first child is only
      a girl because he had a dream &
      oldest sister has been chosen

by God   father will give her life
   as Abraham did Isaac   father
      will show his faith even if he must
         also climb mountaintop & sacrifice

this life upon Almighty's altar
   to become the most blessed of men
      by God, the good & loyal servant
      amen

in the years afterward when
   father would tell this story in his church
      only more *amens* would follow but now

I wonder what mother thought back
   pressed against wooden pew   head bowed
      listening to those long nine months
      of belly growing

now taken because of the words
   this man she has married
      says he has seen in the dark
         each night when she must give

her body to him to be fruitful
   & multiply again   but oh
      how can she want to hold
         more of what she knows is most

precious   what he would give
   away so easily as if expendable
      an endless supply like the leftover bits

of food she scrapes from these Americans'
   half-finished plates & into garbage bin
      every night at workday's end
            before coming home to him again?

PROVERBS OF MY FATHER'S VILLAGE

he may have learned
from his own father
or any other stifled man

in his tribe that holding silence
close is a necessary
breathing thing

pushing words down
prevents pain

& if you choke
down the bile

rising it will not suffocate
you only fester cancerous

inside counting down
the time until you
become a dead thing

but outside you
will still be
a man

JUDGES

he tells them   his American children   how when he was their
age he had to walk two miles up hill to school after hunting
the meat they would eat that day   after fetching the water
they would use that day   after working the fields long hours
before the sun had even risen   then after staying late to finish
homework otherwise there would not be enough light
chalk or slate he would walk those two miles back home to
hunt fetch water plant dig or harvest some more whatever
needed to be done   because it was not just working twice as
hard to succeed as these his American black children get to
do but 5 times 10 times 100 times whatever it took   there
were hundreds of them & only one mission one school one
classroom one chance to be the best & impress the western
missionaries & get sponsored & get out & become something
but they do not understand his American children how
there was no second chance if his trap sprung empty
of prey they would not eat that night   it was winner take all
& he took even if there would be nothing left behind   you
never looked back only forward move forward to succeed
competition was the only thing & winning was everything
but still his American children say: *why does everything have
to be a competition, why do you have to be so hard* & he wonders
how they can want him softer when there is no room for
softness   can they not see such a thing was death where he
comes from   if he did not make himself so hard he would
not have pushed past them all for that one chance to win
escape & he did escape but they   his American children   all
they say is *can you not just love us   can you not just take us back
to Uganda to visit so we can know ourselves learn who we are &
how to love ourselves*   love   !?!   had he not taken them out of
Amin's genocide out of love & given them running water
free speech the right to vote a democracy & playing field
that had seemed level all 100% guaranteed by life   liberty &
the pursuit of happiness when back in Uganda 3 of 5 of them
would be dead already from war disease or famine   dear God

had he not done enough   had he not been enough   had he
not tried his best   had he not brought them here to safety
had he not survived   were they not all still alive

DEUTERONOMY

we have been taught
that we must not

speak we
must not see

each other
we would

want to speak then &
if we want

love from the
father we must

put out
our eyes we

must shut tight
our mouths we

must only obey

LEVITICUS

at work still when the day rises
again sunlight dipping into your hollowed ribs
you are not eating

grey-haired man my teacher my dark mirror of what
I want & do not want to become
how I have watched you
want me different

genetics will win   you are a scientist   you have told me

morning last
I found you at your work
house so dust-coated
I could not breathe
the deer eating your overgrown grass

what does this make us
your children
when your work is
the only thing when you cannot hear
the words we hurl against the shuttered window
that is your life

please take care of yourself

that day we found you in the street fallen unconscious
eyes blooded shut
nose so broken you could not breathe &
you would not get help
how you said

if I am going to die from this I would
 already be dead

the door to your office closed behind you &
we could hear the chirp of your computer more alive
than the drone of our voices
asking you to try

STOMACH

at dinner   the air ices
  with secrets   the scrape

  of silver against china a cold hardness
cutting through   that which   we do not say

      in my lap my hands rehearse
         their plunging dance down my

  throat   that willled nothingness
    carving the warm spot

      of father's favorite into my shape
    & not my light-skinned sister's as

      I stand & father slides
    my full plate onto his own   says

      back home in Amin's war   if I ever left
    the fire   my food would be gone by

  my return   stolen by
one of the others in the hunger

    for that   of which
there was   never enough

EARS

the leftover cake is temptation   Satan
   offering Christ the world in a water glass.

   that hot desert day   three times I am lured
     out of bed to open my mouth wide

to the sweet thing   my father sleeping
   down the hall his words no shield

the worst thing to happen to a woman
   is to get fat & lose her looks

I am slicing another sliver &
   swallowing   pink sugar stuck against

pink tongue   floor felled crumbs
   like manna sprung from heaven

& if you need proof just look at your mother
   father in the doorway   something hard

in his hand to beat me with
   & you are shaping up to be just like her

you do not need to eat so much
   until I obey him   in my disappearance

to become wanted filling myself up with
   smoke as if it were the breath of life

kissed into the first man as God's own good truth
   but now I know there are worse

things—like holding close what will destroy me
   being with men who beat me

down accordingly   my baby boy on visitation
    with one of them   his father

his bruises afterward

FIRST & SECOND CROWNS: A REVERSE PANTOUM FOR TWO VOICES

blessed be the mother who does not hit
    now   even though it is light & she says
        she playing miss so&so when *stop*
            I say the memory of when it was not   the sounding

of whip   cracked loud &
    blessed be the mother who does not hit   now
to match the echo of father's—
    . . . & she not playing missy so—so *stop!*

of words cutting my body
of whip cracked loud
        shuddering tense though older
           to match the echo of (the) father

            now   understanding
                        of words cutting my body
            they are who they are
                        shuddering tense though older

        from a home that is not mine
                    now   understanding
                how much I want
                        they are who they are

                to make absence into a known thing
                    from a home that is not mine
                & the universe is in her listening
                    how much I want

& if I know to see I will find
      the making of absence into a known thing
            unable to be   what is the broken done   moved?
        & in her listening   is the universe

                    arms spread wide open
& if I know to see I will find
        after all this after everything
moved   what is unable to be broken

    in the repeating
                arms spread wide open
                        in the breaking   the rising
                after all this after everything

the resonance of this one constant thing
        in the repeating
                        in the living
                        in the breaking   in the rising

BLOOD

years later when my father is dying
& packing up his house
for sale I find the last picture

taken of my family before
the breaking apart my father
sits beside my aunt nestled

knee to knee my youngest sister's arms flung
over them both to hug
my only brother atop his other leg

my mother stands far
left in the opposite corner
my two older sisters
& myself between

my mother does not smile
my father's smile is brilliant
my aunt's satisfied & I finally understand

why people would look at her & not
my mother when telling my father

your wife is so beautiful

ACTS OF ERASURE IN THE COUNTRY
OF NAMELESS WOMEN

after 20 years in America
cleaning their house & cooking
their food & washing their
dishes & doing their laundry

by hand while
keeping the rest of their house
their yard & their children in spotless
order aunt had earned nothing

from my parents—not money
not social security   401K   insurance   emergency
healthcare nor regular—not house nor car
nor any other thing valued in this world

so when father would look down
from his newly remodeled by remortgage million dollar
house & tell her to *count her blessings*
she was rich in family & the love of his

children I could not understand
but she understood

she held in her hand
the still-beating life force of the universe
to be split apart with the sounding

of her whispered account
of every wrong father
done to her

for is not history
littered with the stories
of desperate people close to the edge
& crossing west who

when overcome by hunger
& cold with nothing
left but ability to also cross
that thin red line

took knives to one another
to wear the skin become fur
eat of the body become flesh
drink of the blood become wine?

RIB

between his stomach
   and his heart

that place
    taken from

other animals
    and eaten

with barbecue
    and applesauce

licked clean
    and then thrown

to the dog

LEGS

how in her looking
  back to hold
memory close Lot's wife

  did not worry   rooted
to the ground by
  frozen pillared legs

strange desert mermaid

of coming winds to
  sweep salted flesh
away to nothing

  disappeared

long before being
  turned to salt she

had never
  even owned

  a name

FIGURE 2: MARY, CALLED GIRL
MATERIALS: BLOOD & DARKNESS

surely it was not
your choice to spread your legs

& push   here on this dirty
straw & earth

among the piss & stink
of these animals surely

this was not the birth
plan you had dreamed

as a young girl swaddling
your dolls in your mother's linens

nor was this the man
nor the love

you had breathed
when watching your

oldest sister sneak out late
at night to kiss the brother of the boy

you liked under the inked blackness
of the desert night blurring their bodies

together in a twisting
moaning that wettened

the small space
between your legs &

they had come to you then   the three
shining bright with anticipation &

joy to announce your future
erased from this touch

because you were blessed among women amen

so why then should this moment be
any different when you had never even no not once

been given a choice if you wanted to hold this life
within your body at all?

FIGURE 3: LA PIÈTA
MATERIALS: BREATH & AIR

alternative title: how I know
you and shorty are
black—

in the only pictures
that survive

you are holding
your son

& he is
dying

FIGURE 4: PIÈTA II, BLACK BODY AS CRUCIFIX PATTERNED WITH A FIELD OF SKITTLES CROSSED WITH SEVEN-UP AGAINST A BLOOD RED SKY
MATERIALS: WHITE CONCRETE & LEAD

when I was a little girl you
& I were the best of friends dear father
as I followed you down
the long test-tubed flanked aisles
of your laboratory funded
by the same people who had enslaved
your ancestors and bankrupted your country and
would deny them the medicines
you were discovering   still following
you in stores   still sending cops
to watch our house *because those niggers*
have been up to no good since they moved to our town

I wanted to know *why*
and wrote down everything you said
as truth until I began to think
for myself and you couldn't have that
so you began to beat
at me like a housewife does a stain
as if that would get the education out

the doctors have said you will
spend this year dying
and I want to tell you
so many things   but yesterday
they let free that white man who killed
the brown boy just because he was brown
and the day before that they took away
the protections for our right to vote   and the day
before that they released
a study saying the radiation

from the nuclear disaster exploded
in Japan has already jumped
in the water   swum across the ocean—
up through our faucets   our hoses   into
our earth   plants & animals   our bodies
now dying   infected already
and there is not enough
medicine for everyone
and you know who there
will not be enough for—

this morning I had to stop
while doing my yoga and curl
into a ball hold myself to keep
from shaking   all day long
I've felt terrified little spasms
down my spine and central nervous
system as I remembered
taking my seven-month-old son for
our daily walk because
he loves *outside! outside!*
and I love him & walking with him
pressed against my body
still feeling my bones realigning
muscles unwinding from giving birth
to him   carrying him
and the old white man who lives
in the house on the corner yelled
he would shoot us like that other white man shot
the little brown boy just because
we are brown too   and
all I could do was just think *breathe*
        breathe

there are other people's small horrors too:
a friend who is trying to get pregnant
another miscarriage
says it feels like

meeting a ghost without
ever having met
the person before

and I just want you
my father   to protect
me   teach me how to protect my son
because they have put in a law
that says the last man standing can say
I felt threatened and shoot
to kill and then walk free

and they always say they are threatened of us

and they have taken away
that other law that says they cannot
step in front of our path to
the voting house and stop us

and they have never stopped trying to stop us

and I wonder what is
to stop them from firing
knowing their whiteness
is their ticket to
not guilty
to be set free of
having to feel the rage
of having a man
who looks like you
in their white
house again

III.

I am looking for my body
—Suḥeir Hammad, *Breaking Poems*

FIGURE 5: PIÈTA III, AFTER I WATCH THE VIDEO OF WHITE WOMAN AMY COOPER CHANNELING CAROLYN BRYANT DONHOM IN CENTRAL PARK IN NEW YORK CITY I HAVE A NIGHTMARE AND WAKE IN COLD SWEAT BECAUSE ALL I CAN SEE IS YOUR BROKEN SIX-YEAR-OLD FACE SMASHED IN PULPED AND BLOODY LIKE EMMETT TILL'S

MATERIALS: HISTORY & FEAR

and in six more years   I wonder   will
you be walking peacefully in a park   perhaps while
doing something you love   radiant and shining
in your free black boy joy   perhaps
when a white man or woman who feels most definitely
they can violate you   or at the very least
if too tired   call 911 and perform oscar-worthy
white-teared shaken victim   clicked on say *action!* knowing
as evidence   as history nearly always shows
who will be heard and what will happen
in all likelihood   after these
few minutes   between their hanging
up and blue flashed arrival   that will
most likely be your last

MOUTH II

    & at night I dream of
the lions   they chase &

    lurk below   they
jump up   climb & kill

I have never seen a live one
   but my mother

   now   she tells me
how   the lions would prowl

  her village & attack
       the pythons also

    it would take ten men to kill
each one *which was worse?*

   I ask her *it's hard
to say* she tells me *with*

    *the lions you would find the dead
later   mangled   eaten*

    *but you could tell whose body
parts could be buried   with*

   *the snakes there would be
nothing left*
                  just questions

another
   disappearance

FIGURE 6: THE NAMELESS WOMEN AS A CATEGORY IN ABC'S *JEOPARDY!*: A PARTIAL LIST
MATERIALS: ECHO & SOUND

and when he comes with
his visions & show of might
your sons must follow
leaving

the fields fallow
even though the dry season
is coming even though

the buzzards who wear the skins
of men are coming circling you

the nameless women
left behind to do
what must be done

how your husband will destroy you if you understand your value

how when your father is trapped he will try to sell you

you are a refugee
girl small & starving

& when he sees you are beautiful
he wants & he takes
& you become his

your legs spread wide by his wrinkled hands
in the twilight of his fields

your belly swelled full
with his food &

his seed

how when your father desires he will offer you to other men

how when other men desire   they will call you whore and cast you out

    your husband will take
        your son on a camping trip &
    try to kill him
        & say a voice told him
    to do it

how if you have daughters they will be disappeared from the story

how your rape & destruction are expected asides in violences of men

        & sometimes everyone
          in your entire village
       is wiped out

        & when you look for
          remnants
       all that will be left is

       the slow falling of ash
         of smoke
       like scattered paper torn
       like snow

FIGURE 7: THE NAMELESS WOMEN AS A CATEGORY IN ABC'S *JEOPARDY!*: APPENDIX ANSWER KEY
MATERIALS: ERASURE & LOSS

1. who are the mothers & wives & daughters & sisters of his 12 disciples

2. who is Vashti most gracious high queen & empress of nations

3. who are Lot's daughters & their father's plot to sell them into prostitution to cover his losses

4. who is Ruth

5. who is Mary Magdalene a woman of great honor & worth

6. who are the daughters of the Levite

7. who is Sarah mother of nations who is given exactly 5 lines to speak in the text

8. who are all the nameless women

9. who are all the nameless women

10. who are all the nameless women

11. who are all the nameless women

12. who are all the nameless women

FIGURE 8: RUTH AS THE NAMELESS BLACK GIRLS
AND WOMEN WHO FLEW BECAUSE THEY COULD
NOT SWIM ACROSS THE WATER OF THE MIDDLE
PASSAGE IN THE LATE 18TH CENTURY WHEN
THROWN OVERBOARD, ALIVE AND CHAINED,
FROM BRITISH SLAVE SHIPS FOR COLLECTION OF
THE INSURANCE MONEY BY BRITISH CAPTAINS
WHO HAD DONE THE SAME TO THEIR ANIMAL
CARGOES WITHOUT ANY LEGAL REPERCUSSIONS
AND THOUGHT THEY COULD DO THE SAME
TO HUMAN BEINGS BECAUSE BLACK AND
THEREFORE NOT HUMAN OR EVEN ANIMAL
BUT ONLY THINGS/CARGO AS REMEMBERED
BY THOSE WHO SURVIVED ENSLAVEMENT FOR
GENERATIONS IN AMERICA AND STILL REMAIN
THE ACCEPTED PREY OF WHITE MEN WITH GUNS
WHO SOMETIMES HAVE BADGES
MATERIALS: UNKNOWN

and yet even the animals in your countries now have laws
making their killings a crime punishable by money

&

time

BREATH II

in Nebraska they always stop me
pull me out of line &
give me the extra pat down

while my five-year-old son watches worried
what's happening mama? why they touching you?
& I say *nothing just part of their job* as they
open his tiny Thomas the Train suitcase & rifle

through his toys each one casually taken apart
then put back together before turning back to me to fist
their fingers through my hair that I have decided not to straighten
this day like I usually do when traveling to avoid this moment
because today I have decided to be
myself & not pander to them to protect myself

today I want to be a person

which is not to say that I don't want to be black or woman
I love being black & woman but I want them to see black & woman
means person like I know black & woman
means person like I know black & woman
means person like I know black & woman

what they doing mama? are they hurting you?
baby boy is asking again & I say
nothing pay them no mind
swallowing the rage rising

because if I speak up however soft however *articulate*
they will marvel they will see black & woman not
person & think black & woman & angry
& calling cops &
escalating & I do not want to die today
in front of my five-year-old son like black

mothers & sons & daughters & fathers who look like me
have been made dead by white folk who look like them
here for centuries so I let it go & stand still &feel the sounding

of those century's long line of white hands touching
on black bodies that do not want to
be touched but had no choice until
we are let go

now late & running through with car seat
& purse & suitcases & computer banging
clumsily against my body &
the only other brown

passenger afro a sunned halo among this cloud
of white is already being pulled out for her turn to be clutched
at with their searching hands so
when I hear my son say *I miss home*

I know it is not the beach or mountains
he means or even the sunshine as he
sinks under the cold whiteness here
sky thrown & bone known deep in the body

but the ability to just walk
through without being
pulled out

as if we are just like everybody else
just any other mother & a son
getting on a plane to go see grandpa

BREATH III

sometimes   father   now when you are
        old & shrunken & dying
            & are packing up your shining new house for sale
                because you cannot work
      & do not have enough money

stop to pick up a treasured object & smile
      I see the light in your eyes & imagine
   you a boy again of four or five excited
           having earned enough money
              to pay your school fees & learn

the head of the class the best
       runner you have been called to the headmaster's
office for reward & told
        you are good for a native but

you will never be as good as us
   British you are one of the savages,
      subhuman a lesser species

  there would have been
quotations from Darwin

I want to tell the little boy
      you were then *run keep running*
        away from learning their hate
   of you as right their values
      which are nothing
        like yours but instead I see you look

     around at this white china & white
  furniture this white marble
two-story palace & you think
  some day you will have all this

too some day you will be
best of all some day
you will *show them*

BREATH IV

forty years later &
the police are still stopping you
father as you walk this block
around your American home back bent
skin hung thin from this disease
that is killing you

we need to see your ID where
are you going where are you from

you are an African
man you think you have
rights you do not
answer you
are proud

we watch the news
we say the names we know
we are black in America we are still

thankful each time
when all they do
is ask their questions

when they do
not shoot

SKIN: THE ONLY BLACK GIRL IN SCHOOL

I.

I was watched
  like a dog with two heads, strange
unseen thing bought to amuse

  their hands made into bird claws
clutching at my hair
      it's like a Brillo pad.
      why is it so curly?

how much louder
  would they have been had I not flailed
a reminder among them
  of that which should not be said

I did not yet
  know all they saw
was my skin

II.

they tell me there are no great black ones
  but I bring them my Baldwin heart anyway

      no one will buy nigger stories   he says
      write something else

in their classrooms I taste only silence
  the gray food of their ghosts

all that long winter   they come
  layering ethered white bodies over mine

until they tell me I am different   not
  like the others   I am one of *them*

the white hood of his costume covers
   all but his eyes   his white robe
the rest of his body

he is no longer my friend
  late night conversations &
coffee-fueled homework sessions

now he is a fist clenched to punch
   out the stars & swallow
the blackness
  whole

before this place
  I'd have called myself
a girl beautiful
  & strong   now I am
an empty decaying thing

a black bird blinded
   in winter's
glare mistaking false glass
  for one true thing &
falling hard broken
   & avalanched
with whitened snow

      you can't come over anymore
      my mother doesn't like it

their words are flies pricking at
  at my submerged bird body

    I'm not allowed around
      people like you

buzzing bellies full
  they keep
biting they are
  never satisfied

FIGURE 9: RUTH AS A BLACK GIRL WALKING AMONG THE NAMELESS BLACK WOMEN DISAPPEARED BETWEEN 1619 AND THE PRESENT BY GREAT BRITAIN AND THE AMERICAS
MATERIALS: ECHO & SOUND

I used to think when white men
saw me they

                                                                saw me
                                                                    a person

                    equal

            not a black slave
                    thing
bought
    for their
pleasure

                            to beat up
                                & tie up

        stick
            their penis

                    & other objects
                        into

                    until they came
                        & were finished

never mind your screaming
        or hunger strike

                                        they would have cut out
                                        your tongue

            you would have
                been forcefed

                    or the other

                                        starving
                                  denied food till near
            dead & not strong

                                        enough to fight them
                                              off your body
they would not even need
      their chains   but for their

                        always wanting

      you pressed so tight
            between hard iron   you almost suffocate
                                              alone in their darkness

                  until they next want
                        to use you again

      & oh the whips
                                        to beat you with until

you whisper yes
            master yes

                                              please master
                  as they could do
                  anywhere
                              at any time

                  to any one
                  of us

for 300 years
      from 1619 to 1865

                        by their law
                        & their bible

                                        & from 1865 to 1965
                              by rope & tree

74

    & from 1965
       to now

          because white
           boys will be boys

              because isn't that
                what all women

  are good
for anyway

  no matter their
      color skin

           & us always

        the least
            protected
        of all?

FIGURE 10: SELF-PORTRAIT AS RUTH
MATERIALS: UNKNOWN

how do I speak in this language that is not mine

how do I become what I have not been taught

how do I remember what is erased

how do I speak in this language of their violence that is not mine

how do I find what is lost

how do I dream in my language that I do not know

how can I hear the ancestors if I cannot

how do I speak in this language of their violence that has erased my own

what is beyond this palimpsest

how do I find my body

IV.

What is it like to be so free?

—Ladan Osman, *Exiles of Eden*

EXODUS II: SURVIVOR'S WALK

this my heart he does spoon—
   a dull-edged, rusted almost circle of silver—
from within my rib cage

   & sucks the marrow out hard
raw   his teeth & lips dripped red
   by this four chambered organ still pumping

inside the press of his fingers
   bite by bite leeching its hard won
labors to fuel his parasite life until

   nothing left but my rhythm still live
still moving I understand
   how long after our own bones become

ashes become dust
   will rise the sounding of this
most ancient terrible thing

FIGURE 11: SELF–PORTRAIT AS FIRE AND OSHUN
MATERIALS: WATER

a year after the last time he has come back
& I have left him—his markings on my body

deepened from darkened bruise to press
within nerve tendon & bone
I meet a friend for dinner

pulled one by one from the oyster mouth
of her unclasped red handbag
she gives me lemons   yellow pearls raw
in the press of becoming

& I understand how the first creation
was not of clay & newborn pink flesh

but out of black
water & fire ashed
embers ended
that single
red–risen flame

PIÈTA IV: REVELATIONS

you sing the red of our separation
   before you   his skilled deception—a part
played endless curtained with your birth
    when I woke & felt his fisted shadow rising
my body pushed rough
    in fitted shape to hold him soft
you deserve better   hatched inside
    the promise of warm safety
now shuttled between without words
    your wants unheard   your missing
of my milk & body a terrible
    howl echoed within my still-opened womb

that day when you pushed through them & out
slid up to rest your tiny hands on my chest
look up at me

latch your lips to my breast & receive more
than your life from my body
I held your soft warm realness & wished you safe
again inside instead of this place
& you the target for white folks'
stand your ground black kid hunting

in my not knowing
how fear rises in matched level with love
deepening I dreamed only the unbearable joy
of your tiny arms pressed around

but then there must be this also: the empty
confusion when apart from you
mind fretted & body sick tiptoeing nights

of making sure you still draw breath wanting
to protect you from what you do not know
& will hurt you while sleeping even

while knowing were I able
to do this each second of each day
of all your life it still would not be enough

formed of my cells formed
of my mother's cells inside

my body memory flowing
back into my body my brain

changed, the scientists say

when you are becoming
from my becoming
from her becoming
in line with another & the next &

even after your long push

through water   the bloodied opening

into this world this will remain:

your cells   the code of
your life   you rest

here abide in me

how you hold   what is being held   is there hurt
is there tired   is there healing   a pause to rest
or ignore the twisting   with the press of
the weight   of   what is   being
held to support   to create movement   pressure points
connecting flow oxygen   blood energy   of the body family
the direction of   whole   the becoming of
movement   the central definition of   life   of   breath

FIGURE 12: PORTRAIT OF BLACK JESUS
AS THE NAMING OF THE GHOSTS
MATERIALS: WATER & MEMORY

be

the walking on   the dam lifted   the blue waters
again free flowing

be

their violence   our disappeared
their theft ongoing made known
be

the risen black
the risen black
be

mother   heart stopped   silver
stent stuttered into blued life
be

the first shrug of weary shoulders
from the   crossed   wooden   weight   be

how in the final ebbing he is small   my

father   *be—*

blue comfort   be ocean
be

the history of red   flamed
the sharp that was not spared   skinstitched   be

the putting   away
the laying it   down
be

the leaving
he who does harm

                                                                be

                                        absence made whole in
            the knowing   of the body family

                                                                be

the blue hour   the midnight watching   rise & fall
            of the newborn's breath   be

    the flood   be   not a   sinking sight but
            skipped blue like a green thing made   be

NOTES

In the Christian Bible, Ruth is the daughter-in-law of Naomi, who follows Naomi to look for safety after the war. Homeless, poor, and widowed, Ruth and Naomi survive as exiles in a foreign land. Eventually, in the alien country, Ruth marries and becomes the Matriarch of the House of Jesse who begat David who begat Mary Mother of God. As the daughter of people who fled violence to find safety in a foreign land myself, Ruth haunts me. As I tried to make sense of my family's story of surviving genocide and what it means to be a stranger in a strange land, as I tried to understand what this experience means for so many women and girls around the world, not just in my own culture, Ruth walked with me.

"Khuhu" is the Lugisu word for grandmother.

The poem "Figure 1: Portrait of Ruth Understanding What Became of Eve in the Garden as Her Body as War. *Materials: Wind & Sand*" is after the poem "On Earth We're Briefly Gorgeous," by Ocean Vuong.

The poem "Deuteronomy" is after the poem "We Real Cool" by Gwendolyn Brooks.

The poem "Figure 4: Pièta II Black Body as Crucifix Patterned with a Field of Skittles Crossed with Seven-UP Against A Blood Red Sky. *Materials: White Concrete & Lead*" was written after the death of, and for Trayvon Martin, who was murdered by George Zimmerman on the sidewalk outside his own home after going to the store to buy Skittles.

The poem "Figure 5: Pièta III, after I Watch the Video of White Woman Amy Cooper Channeling Carolyn Bryant Donhom in Central Park in New York City I Have a Nightmare and Wake in Cold Sweat because All I Can See Is Your Broken Six-Year-Old Face Smashed in Pulped and Bloody Like Emmett Till's, *Materials: History & Fear*" is written after the poem "A Small Needful Fact," by Ross Gay, which mourns the death of Eric Garner.

I would like to express my gratitude to the journals that have published poems from this collection, sometimes in earlier forms or under different titles:

"Mouth," published in *Ruminate Literary Journal.*

"Exodus: Father's American Superheroes," published in *Ruminate Literary Journal.*

"Breath I," published in *Connotation Press.*

"Job (Survivor's Guilt)" published in the *Nasty Women Poets Anthology* and *Ruminate Literary Journal.*

"Naomi after the War," published in *Connotation Press.*

"Lamentations," published in *U City Review.*

"Refugee Mind," published in *Connotation Press.*

"Chronicles (of a Violence Foretold)," published in *Literary Mama.*

"Numbers," published in *Kalyani Magazine.*

"Mother after the War Is Still Talking to the Dead," published in *Connotation Press.*

"Judges," published in *The Sun.*

"Deuteronomy," published in *Salamander Literary Journal.*

"Ears," published in *Tinderbox Literary Journal.*

"Rib," published in *North American Review.*

"Legs," published in *Foundry Literary Journal.*

"Mouth II," published in *U City Review.*

"Breath II," published in *Connotation Press.*

"Breath III," published in *Connotation Press.*

"Skin: The Only Black Girl in School," published in *Potluck Magazine.*

"Exodus II: Survivor's Walk," published in *Potluck Magazine.*

"Figure 11: Self-Portrait as Fire and Oshun. *Materials: Water,*" published in *Potluck Magazine.*

ACKNOWLEDGMENTS

I thank God for this life.

Many, many thanks to my son Aslan, my parents, my family, and my friends.

I am immensely thankful to the intellectual and creative spaces that have nurtured me over the years: Northwestern University, New York University's Graduate Creative Writing Program, the Kimbilio Center for African American Fiction, the African Poetry Book Fund, the National Endowment for the Arts, the Barbara Deming Memorial Fund for Women Writers, the Awesome Foundation, SPACE at Ryder Farm, VONA Voices, Crescendo Lit, the Fulbright program, and Cave Canem.

It would be impossible to mention by name all the wonderful, dedicated people involved with these programs, the peers who have inspired me artistically, or the friends have held me in friendship as I wrote this book, but I would like to thank Ruth Forman, Marco Abel, Kwame Dawes, Matthew Shenoda, Chris Abani, Aricka Foreman, Camille Rankine, Hafizah Geter, Ladan Osman, Mahtem Shiferraw, Ashley Strosnider, Joy Castro, Timothy Schaffert, Jamie Pachino, Amelia Montes, Jeannette Jones, Grace Bauer, Bernardine Evaristo, Jennine Capó Crucet, Stacey Waite, Kwakiutl Dreher, Eve L. Ewing, Anjali Enjeti, Carolyn Kellog, Nate Marshall, Deborah Landau, Chuck Wachtel, Brian Morton, Alice Kang, Dai Shizuka, Emily Kazyak, James Brunton, Mary McMyne, Gila Berryman, Maaza Mengiste, Edie Rhoads, Kristin Dunn, Marisela Mendoza, Annalyn Hallas, Kera Bolonik, Laurie Muchnick, Lynne Pitts, Jenée Desmond-Harris, Ilana Masad, Solmaz Sharif, Kirsten West Savali, and Meghan Sullivan. I would like to thank my incredible students who inspire me regularly with their excitement and talent. Thank you also to the University of Nebraska–Lincoln, the place that allowed me to be still and do the work. Thank you to Ashon Crawley for his beautiful artwork.

Thanks also to the indefatigable Sarah Bowlin, you are amazing, and to the rare unicorn Maya Marshall and Haymarket Books—I could not be happier with this home for *The Body Family.*

This book is dedicated to those disappeared from the violence of genocide and war—specifically to the innocent women and children caught in these violences of men.

ABOUT THE AUTHOR

Hope Wabuke is a Ugandan American poet, essayist, and critic. She is the author of the chapbooks *her*, *The Leaving*, and *Movement No.1: Trains*. Hope has received fellowships and awards from the National Endowment for the Arts, the National Book Critics Circle, *The New York Times* Foundation, the Barbara Deming Memorial Fund for Women Writers, Cave Canem, the Awesome Foundation, Yale University's THREAD Writer's Program, the Poetry Foundation, and the Voices of Our Nations Arts Foundation (VONA). She is an assistant professor of English at the University of Nebraska–Lincoln, and writes literary and cultural criticism for NPR.

ABOUT HAYMARKET BOOKS

Haymarket Books is a radical, independent, nonprofit book publisher based in Chicago.

Our mission is to publish books that contribute to struggles for social and economic justice. We strive to make our books a vibrant and organic part of social movements and the education and development of a critical, engaged, international left.

We take inspiration and courage from our namesakes, the Haymarket martyrs, who gave their lives fighting for a better world. Their 1886 struggle for the eight-hour day—which gave us May Day, the international workers' holiday—reminds workers around the world that ordinary people can organize and struggle for their own liberation. These struggles continue today across the globe—struggles against oppression, exploitation, poverty, and war.

Since our founding in 2001, Haymarket Books has published more than five hundred titles. Radically independent, we seek to drive a wedge into the risk-averse world of corporate book publishing. Our authors include Noam Chomsky, Arundhati Roy, Rebecca Solnit, Angela Y. Davis, Howard Zinn, Amy Goodman, Wallace Shawn, Mike Davis, Winona LaDuke, Ilan Pappé, Richard Wolff, Dave Zirin, Keeanga-Yamahtta Taylor, Nick Turse, Dahr Jamail, David Barsamian, Elizabeth Laird, Amira Hass, Mark Steel, Avi Lewis, Naomi Klein, and Neil Davidson. We are also the trade publishers of the acclaimed Historical Materialism Book Series and of Dispatch Books.